The Peace of God

A Place to Live and Experience

Albert Friend

The Peace of God

Scripture quotations are taken from The
Message Bible, The King James Version,
And The New Living Translation.

Some scripture quotations are the author's
Paraphrase.

Published in the United States of America by
Friend Family Ministries Publications
1601 Hamilton-Richmond Road
Hamilton, Ohio 45013

Editorial Consultant: Nancy Ulrich

ISBN 0-9767524-1-7

Library of Congress Control Number 2005903691

The Peace of God
A Place to Live and Experience

Table of Contents

Peace!

Be Still!

The wind and the sea obey Him.
Mark 4:39-41

Preface

The Message Bible calls God's peace, **God's wholeness**.

"Don't fret or worry. Rather than worrying, pray. Let petitions and praises shape your worries into prayers. Let God know your concerns. Before you know it, a sense of **God's wholeness** and peace will come and settle you down. It's wonderful when Christ displaces worry from the center of your life." Philippians 4:6-7

You need to believe that God's love for you is so strong that you can cast all your cares on Him (1 Pet. 5:7). He wants you to do this. Give God what He wants. When you cast your cares upon Him, God will fill you with His peace. Then, you will not worry. You will just love Him back as you perform His word in your life. Remember! This peace comes at the *beginning* of your trial. God speaks to you in the *beginning* of your trial. He speaks Romans 8:28, "And we know that all things work together for good to them that love God, to them who are the called according to his purpose." God says, "Everything is going to be all right!"

God is a spirit. He is everywhere. With this knowledge, we can understand that God fills all the space around us at all times. In Him we live, move, and have our being (Acts 17:28). God can take care of you as though you were the only one in the universe He had to care for.

I challenge you to read this book. Study it and apply it. As you do, expect to receive God's peace in your heart.

Chapter 1

Faith in God's Love Produces Peace

You cannot live life without problems. I have found that we all get strength through the things we resist. The more we resist the stronger we get.

For example, with physical exercise we resist gravity by walking, running, swimming and doing many other things. Resisting gravity causes our bodies to become strong. Then, we become healthy and are able to handle our physical problems.

There are also problems that we cannot grab with our physical hands. These are spiritual battles. Sometimes we wish we could get hold of them with our two hands, but we can't. These problems are elusive. We seem to be unable to get hold of them. There is a way, however. We can pray.

The book in your hands is about how to build yourself strong in the Lord with His power and His might through prayer using the word of God (Eph. 6:10).

These are spiritual exercises that you can perform to win the victory over your enemy.

We all think in pictures; we do not think in words. When a person talks to us, we see a "picture" of the words he is saying. We do not see the letters of the alphabet spelling out the spoken words.

There are pictures of things I have never seen with my mind, therefore, I do not know they exist. I conclude from this that all living goes on in the mind. I conclude also that "better thinking means better living." You need muscle in your mind to resist the devil's spiritual wickedness in high places (Eph. 6:12). The muscle in your mind becomes stronger because you

> **Better Thinking means better living.**

believe in God's integrity. He cannot lie. His word cannot fail. You can trust every word He has spoken. In the end you win!

I have had some thoughts growing in me for many years. I have taken a part of my harvest and used it for my immediate needs. There has always been more harvest than I needed personally, so I have returned it to reseed the field. I share my harvest with others. In this book, I want to sow into you and plant into your heart some seed. Please accept it from the God who gave the increase.

There is no way for you to get God's peace without reading about it in the Bible. We all get lazy when we are reading unless what we read is appealing to us. Do not let your mind get lazy and wander away from your subject. Keep God's peace in focus. Give heed to your awareness level because this is where it will appear as a gift from God. Keep awake and alert until you activate God's peace in your heart. You must have the "want to" in you or it will not happen. God monitors your "want to."

The Way to Peace

God's peace is a promise in His word for you to believe. Your faith in this promise will come by hearing the word spoken by God, the word that I will be ministering to you in this book. All God's promises come to you through faith in His word.

I want to show you the way to peace. God has sent me to you so that you may believe in His peace.

Without faith it is impossible to get anything from God (Heb. 11:6). If you do not believe God's word, God's peace will have no affect on your life. You will still be at war with yourself.

There is no back door to yesterday that allows you to change what has happened to you. There is nothing coming in your front door that you can look forward to that will lift your load. The answer to your request for peace is in the "today." Today, God is offering you His peace. He is doing it through the Prince of Peace, the one whose coming into the world was heralded by angels with the words, "Peace on earth, good will toward men." Jesus is your answer. Have faith in God.

You cannot experience the peace of God while you are living in sin. God will not respond to you. You cannot produce God's peace on your own. You cannot experience God's peace until you call on God's name.

You are not alone in your ignorance about God's peace. The whole world lies in darkness. The great apostle Paul, in his book to the Romans, proves that Jews and Gentiles were all under sin, as he stated in Rom.3:9. Then in 3:17 he said: "God's peace have they not known."

You cannot trust in riches to give you peace. Money will not give you peace when you have lost a loved one through death.

I am coming to you, through this book, to show

you the way to peace as taught by Jesus Christ, the Prince of Peace. He is the light shining in the darkness. The darkness cannot overcome Him. He is the way, the truth, and the life.

God's peace only comes by His spirit because His peace is spiritual. It fills your whole being with peace.

Why do we not have peace? Because we worry.

Why do we worry? Because on our own, we cannot handle some problems in life.

What is our answer to all this? God's peace is our answer. God wants us to be at peace. He wants us to experience His peace at the level of our biggest problem. God's love is God's peace. He sent the "Prince of Peace" to teach us about this peace.

God wants to give you His peace through His promises in the Bible.

Peace is something that comes after the war has been won.

God wants you to have His peace when your battle *starts*. God's peace gives you the feeling that you have already won the battle! You feel as though your battle is already over. STOP! Read that again.

It's TRUE! You can have peace while fighting your battle!

God will give you His peace in your trial's starting moments. He wants you to strike a covenant with Him by casting all your cares

> Knowing that God's word cannot be broken allows the simplest person to become wise.

on Him (1 Pet. 5:7). He wants you to activate your faith in His word. Give God what He wants. Your peace will continue as long as you continue. He will supply you with peace until the battle is won.

How does this happen? You activate God's peace by believing a promise in His word. He wants you to trust in His integrity. Give God what He wants and He will perform His word in you.

Hebrews 11:6 says, "He that cometh to God must believe that He is a rewarder of them that diligently seek Him."

Notice the word "diligently.

Chapter 2

The Peace of God in Times of Sorrow and Grief

The peace of God is a "necessity" in coping with the death of one you love. When you lose someone you love, the loss is overwhelming. The grief is all darkness. Second Corinthians 7:10 says, "The sorrow of the world worketh death." Grief will kill you. There are people who have let grief kill them. They couldn't take the loss. The grief shut down their will to live and they just pined away. They just quit breathing because they felt hopeless. All they wanted to do was die. And die they did.

BUT! There is hope. That hope is in the peace of God that passes all understanding. God, in His all-wise providence, will break through your darkness and bring you His marvelous light. He loves you. He cares about

> The proof that God's word cannot fail lies in the past. Not one word that He has spoken has failed.

you. Man is by far His greatest creation. He wants you to be at peace again, not grieving over the death of the one you love.

The biggest hurdle in this battle is to accept it. When you first get word of the demise of your loved one, your first words are: "Oh, No!" You may repeat it: "NO! NO! NO! NO!" Then you burst into tears. Your resistance brings increased grieving. It is a horrible loss either way. The difference is this. In one you have hope, but in the other you have none. With no hope you have nothing to live for and you want to die. With hope something inside you says, "I will travel through this somehow. I will live on." The person with the hope is trusting in Him who said; "I am the resurrection and the life." His name is Jesus.

When my father died, my heart was full of sorrow. I heard him call my name so I went quickly to his bedside, knowing he was near the end. He was in the hospital and I was alone with him. Immediately, I went for the nurse who summoned the doctor. I stood there with my hand touching the upper left side of his chest, praying as he left this world. My first thoughts were, "My dad is gone. All the knowledge he would speak to me is gone. Never again will I hear his wisdom."

Then I thought of the story he told me about when

his dad, my grandpa Friend, died. My grandpa was about gone but he was making sounds. It was clear to my dad that Grandpa was calling his name. He was calling "Earl," who is my father and Grandpa's oldest son. Dad said he went to his side, put his hands on his cheeks, and stood there praying until Grandpa Friend was gone. The day Dad died, I felt like he wanted to leave me with the same blessing his dad had left him because he called out my name, "Al", his oldest son. Then, he died.

In several conversations we had, dad would tell me of a dream he had. He saw his dad walking through the glade near Friendsville, Maryland. Grandpa was waving his cap to dad as he walked through the wild flowers in the glade. Every time Dad told me this story, he would cry. This was twenty years after Grandpa's death. I was born in 1930, the same year my grandpa, Albert Friend, died. I don't remember ever seeing him.

I handled my father's death well until the day we drove away from the old homestead. Then I broke and wept uncontrollably. I did not realize what I was holding back. Grief overwhelmed me as I drove away, heading for my home.

Twenty years later, I went through a much more

horrible time of grief. I lost my oldest son who was named after me, Albert Lewis Friend Jr. He was 38 years old when he died of an incurable brain tumor. This was, by far, the biggest test of my life.

His battle with this tumor covered a three-year period. I was with him frequently during this time since his wife was in college, studying to be a nurse. When the doctor told them Albert's test results, they wept together and then set their faces toward their future. Kimberly, who we called Kim, would continue her nursing studies so she would be able to take care of their two daughters, Holly and Rachel. Albert determined to commit himself to God and the road He had given him to walk. He set his face toward heaven and told the family, "If God does not choose to heal me, but decides to take me, do not be mad at God."

My son had activated the peace of God at his deepest level.

He resigned the pastorate of his church in Bethel, Ohio and then began to minister with me

Isa 26:3 Thou wilt keep him in perfect peace, whose mind is stayed on thee: because he trusteth in thee.

in our church in Hamilton. He wrote his testimony

in a brochure we published for circulation. I am inserting it here.

On the brochure, there was a picture of a church building on the front page. The title on the front page read as follows:

I FOUND PROBLEMS ON BOTH SIDES OF THE WALLS OF THE CHURCH BUILDING BUT JESUS IS ON BOTH SIDES TOO!

By Albert Friend Jr.

My name is Albert Friend Jr.

You may think it would be much easier to be a Christian if your parents were, or if they may have even been ministers in some church. It is not. More is expected of you even though you are no less or more human than anyone else. I had more judges than fellows, but I had the best examples in my parents. God saved me from my sins. I'm still as human as ever: still with problems to overcome. By God's amazing grace I succeed.

I grew up going to church and found problems on both sides of the walls of the church building. But I learned that my savior was on both sides of the wall too. On July 31, 1989 I went into surgery at the University Hospital in Cincinnati for a brain tumor removal where I learned that Astrocytoma (my case) is an incurable deadly cancer. After surgery I underwent the suggested radiation treatments with little hope of improvement. There was none.

May 31, 1990 I was back in the hospital for another dose of the same thing. Another tumor was removed and I spent another seven days in the hospital, five days in ICU. God provided for my family's needs the entire time. We never did without. Yes we questioned God vehemently, ????? Why God? Why? The answer, "Trust me. I know what I'm doing." "The just shall live by faith and not by sight" (Rom. 1:17 & 2 Cor. 5:17). "Why" is not a faith based question.

I'm sure that one reason why this has happened to me is to make me another witness of what God wants to do for you. You don't need some terrible problem to get you to come to the Lord do you? See and take heed to my witness. God can, will, wants to, take special care of you. He is on both sides of the wall of the church building. God knows about you. He

> Perfect peace is a rare quality. You can achieve it when you keep your mind stayed on Jesus, because your trust is in Him only.

loves you and has great patience. Yes it's amazing grace. And it's yours too.

It has been more than two years since then and there is another tumor. I have committed myself to God again and this time said "No" to the surgeon. God has continuously performed a great miracle in me. *THERE IS NO PAIN!*

Nobody can live life like that without God's help. Join us! We care! We understand! We've been there too. Join us and we'll make it together.

Bio

Albert Friend Jr. is a 37-year-old father of two beautiful daughters, Holly and Rachel. His wife Kim is studying at Miami University, Hamilton Branch, to be a Nurse. He has provided pastoral care in Birdseye, Indiana and Bethel, Ohio. He is now ministering in Hamilton at the Abundant Life Ministries Church. His sickness has made him well known around the world wherever we have missionaries. He is willing to speak wherever asked. His witness is positive and he will minister to anyone with needs. He faces life with an attitude that every day is an extension. For him to live is Christ, to die is gain!

The end of the brochure

Albert once told me about a time when his children were creating noise. They were having fun at night and he couldn't get to sleep. He said, "I just lay there praising God, thanking Him that I could still hear." He walked a straight course, with peace in his heart, until the end.

Kim had to spend a lot of time going to school and studying. I was privileged to be with Albert much of the time when Kim could not. I was his moral support. He loved me and leaned on me. I went with him to his chemotherapy treatments, which caused his hair to fall out. I listened as he told me how he would get a handful of hair in his hand when showering. The chemotherapy didn't work but his hair did grow back. He always looked like a healthy, strong man. The tumor was his big problem.

The progress of the astrocytoma tumor is like turning the lights out one at a time. That was the way it worked with him. I walked with him as the lights started to go out. He was so brave! He kept the peace of God at the deepest level of his life.

Before his last days, we picked up his bed with him in it, and moved him into our home. Then on Sunday evening, November 29, 1992, at about 11pm, our family gathered around his bed. He was laboring hard in his breathing.

Let me insert something here before telling you more. Our family knows the peace of God. We all knew Albert was going to where he belonged. We also knew that we are going to heaven, too, because that is where we belong. We do not belong here. We were not created for this life. We were created to spend eternity in heaven. That's where we are going. We are going home to be with Jesus because that's where we belong.

As Albert was having difficulty breathing someone said, "It's all right, Albert, turn it loose, go on ahead and be with Jesus." He finally took in his last breath. There was an extra long pause and we knew this was it. We all stood there holding our breath. Then he gave one final exhale as with a sound of relief. It was as though he was telling us, "All right, I will go where I belong." We knew then he was gone. Our unselfishness for him then changed to grief. We started to mourn our earthly loss.

When my father died, I held up well, but this time I did not hold up as well or as long. When I did break, I knew the dark grief that gripped me was going to kill me. This time I became desperate. The worldly sorrow was stronger than I was. At times, it would grab me with a death lock. Then I would yell out with a loud voice: "GOD, I THANK YOU FOR 38 YEARS WITH THAT BOY!"

That was my victory. By praising God with a loud voice I was rising above the darkness of unbelief. I was stronger than my adversary. I knew it. I had hope in God. Then I would break into weeping as the black hands of death would go away and leave me alone. It was horrible but I knew God. I knew there was hope. I would continue to praise God until I had activated the peace of God deep within my soul.

Grief can come back. My loss occurred 12 years ago, but as I write this, the same darkness has tried to shut me down. Just telling you my story brings it all back in vivid form. It would be easy to cry right now, but I will take a break and come back later to my writing. I am better now because I know how to restore the peace of God back into my own life. Remember! My son is where he belongs.

There are times while lying in bed at night that I think about him. Then the grief tries to come back on me. But I shake myself loose of it by activating the peace of God. I begin to praise Him and reach for another one of His promises. This time I will quote, "The LORD gives His beloved sleep." Then I will say, "I want to go to sleep, God. Fulfill your word in me." Soon, the peace of God allows me to go to sleep. Praise God for His peace.

Chapter 3

God's Love is the Source of His Peace

Our peace comes from God who loved us enough
to die for us. Be confident that He is watching over
us. His eyes run to and fro throughout the whole
earth (2 Chron. 16:9). He will never leave us nor
forsake us (Heb. 13:5). He has promised us peace.
Peace does not come because we are perfect. Peace
comes because He loves us. He gave His life for
us. That means God is interested in you as an
individual. You are worth more than everything in
the world. If you gained the whole world and lost
your soul what would you have profited?

God will generate
peace in your heart at
the level of your
biggest problem. You
will be amazed.

> God is interested
> in you as an
> individual.

"And the peace of God, which passeth all
understanding, will keep your hearts and minds
through Christ Jesus." Philippians 4:7

Activating God's peace is not an easy thing to do for it calls us to surrender our pride. It calls us to recognize that the peace He gives is greater than ourselves. On the other hand, our pride, tells us that we can work out our own problems when in reality we cannot.

"For none of us liveth to himself, and no man dieth to himself." Romans 14:7

No man is self-sustaining. We need God's peace.

Hebrews 13:5-6 states, "Let your conversation be without covetousness; be content with such things as ye have: for he hath said, 'I will never leave thee, nor forsake thee.' So that we may boldly say, 'The Lord is my helper, I will not fear what man will do unto me.'"

Your attitude toward Hebrews 13:5 is like a valve. The more you open it, the more peace and the less fear you will have.

"There is no fear in love; but perfect love casteth out fear: because fear hath torment. He that feareth is not made perfect in love." 1 John 4:18

You know you have arrived when the peace of God, which passeth all understanding, is keeping your heart and mind in peace through your strong love for Jesus Christ. You feel secure in God and in your giving and getting.

Peace is Not Just an Air Castle

```
PEACE IS A REAL
PLACE TO LIVE
AND EXPERIENCE
```

Peace is not just a topic for discussion. It is a real place in which to live. Peace is not a thing of the past. It is a present help for you in your time of storm. Peace is NOW! Do not let the devil blind you as he did the Jews when Jesus was on earth.

"And when he was come near, he beheld the city, and **wept** over it, Saying, 'If thou hadst known, even thou, at least in this thy day, the **things which belong unto thy peace!** but they are hid from thine eyes.'" Luke 19:41-42

They did not know God's peace. All they knew was the Law which they could not keep. They were never at peace and constantly under condemnation. Jesus poured Himself out to them in things about love and peace. They would not have Him. So it was then that Jesus said, "It's too late. They are hid from thine eyes." Notice, He was weeping when He spoke these words. Never let it be said about you, "Too Late! Too Late!" Learn now about your peace from God.

There was another time that Jesus spoke in the same way. In Matthew 23:37 He said, "O Jerusalem, Jerusalem, thou that killest the prophets, and stonest them which are sent unto thee, how often would I have gathered thy children together, even as a hen gathereth her chickens under her wings, **and ye would not!**"

Here, Jesus gave an example that everyone can understand. He said: "I am like a mother hen who protects her baby chicks under her wings." When the mother hen tucks the chicks under her wings, their eyes are closed. They are safe at rest. They have the peace of God. Jesus wants us to have peace like this.

There are times, though, when we will not let Him. I have watched a child fight sleep. Just when they were about to go to sleep they would jerk and cry aloud so they could stay awake.

I have observed adults fight God's love in the same way. They would begin to understand God's peace. They would begin to rest. Then, however, they would begin to think and take the matter into their own hands again. Instantly, God's peace would be gone.

Jesus wants to give us peace at the level of our biggest problem. He is saying these words to the world today, "I want to but you will not." Let me say it again. God's peace is available on a moment's notice. His peace is present at this very moment.

"God is our refuge and strength, a very present help in trouble." Psalm 46:1

Jesus spoke another time in John 5:39-40 saying, "Search the scriptures; for in them ye think ye have eternal life: and they are they which testify of me. **And ye will not come to me**, that ye might have life."

Oh, if we could only see what God wants to do in us? He has great plans for His people. He wants to form us into the very image of Jesus Christ (Rom. 8:29). He wants us to look like Him, walk like Him, and talk like Him. He wants us to represent Him in the world. He is asking us to come to Him so that we might have this great life in peace. He wants us to come to Him! Give

God has great plans for people.

God what He wants. We should say to Him, "Yes I will! I will come to you. I will accept your calling."

Allow me to show you another thing Jesus said in Luke 4:17-21 "And there was delivered unto him the book of the prophet Esaias. And when he had opened the book, he found the place where it was written, 'The Spirit of the Lord is upon me, because he hath anointed me to preach the gospel to the poor; he hath sent me to heal the brokenhearted, to preach deliverance to the captives, and recovering of sight to the blind, to set at liberty them that are bruised, To preach the acceptable year of the Lord.' And he closed the book, and he gave it again to the minister, and sat down. And the eyes of all them that were in the synagogue were fastened on him. And he began to say unto them, **'This day** is this scripture fulfilled in your ears.'"

The Good News

The poor do not have to be poor anymore.
The brokenhearted do not have to be broken anymore.
The captives do not have to be captive anymore.
The blind do not have to be blind anymore.
The bruised are liberated. They do not have to be bruised anymore.

The unacceptable do not have to feel unaccepted anymore. They are accepted in the beloved.

Have you perceived your potential yet? Are you searching for what you should do to activate God's peace in your heart?

Here is what you should do.

You Must Work the Work of Faith

"Remembering without ceasing **your work of faith,** and labour of love, and patience of hope in our Lord Jesus Christ, in the sight of God and our Father." 1 Thessalonians 1:3

"Wherefore also we pray always for you, that our God would count you worthy of this calling, and fulfill all the good pleasure of his goodness, and **the work of faith** with power."
2 Thessalonians 1:11

Here is the work you must do. You must believe this good news to get its benefits. That's hard to do. It's labor. It's a different type of work, though. What I am saying is found in the Gospel of John. Jesus fed five thousand then He went to the other side of the sea. Some people labored in their boats to get to where Jesus was. On their arrival, Jesus spoke the words that are key to having His love in our biggest problem.

Hear this as recorded in John 6:26-29. "Jesus answered them and said, 'Verily, verily, I say unto you, Ye seek me, not because ye saw the miracles, but because ye did eat of the loaves, and were filled. Labour not for the meat which perisheth, but for that meat which endureth unto everlasting life, which the Son of man will give unto you: for him hath God the Father sealed.' Then said they unto him, 'What will we do, that we might work the works of God?' Jesus answered and said unto them, '**This is the work of God, that ye believe** on him whom he hath sent.'"

Notice what Jesus said. "This is the work of God, that you *believe*."

When you labor to get this faith you will have an enduring faith that keeps you faithful to God. At times this can be hard to do, but there is no other way. I repeat, there is no other way.

"He that cometh to God must believe that He is, and that He is a rewarder of them that diligently seek Him." Hebrews 11:6

Notice the scripture says God is a rewarder. Stay

faithful and never give up. Then, you will have the peace of God for your biggest problem. You will know you have arrived when the peace of God reigns in your heart.

In Mark 11:24 Jesus promised, "Thus I say unto you, What things soever ye want, when ye pray, believe that ye receive them, and ye will have them."

Believing is getting. We must get it freely by His grace (Rom. 3:24). We must either receive it as a gift or do without it.

I gave an earlier copy of this book to a friend of mine who had just been saved. He said my book was easy to read but hard to do. I immediately understood what he meant. He meant he wanted God's peace, but just reading my book didn't give it to him.

Folks, that's what Jesus meant when He said, "This is the work of God, that you believe." There are times when it is not easy to believe and you have to work at it. Yes, you have to work hard at it.

The words Jesus used are, "work of God." It is "work" that God wants us to do. Give God what He wants. Trust in the integrity of His Word.

The Peace of God

Chapter 4

The Peace of God

What is "God's peace"? God's peace is being at peace with God, yourself and others. It is letting Him fight your battles. You can do it.

"Peace" has the following definitions in the dictionary:
1. In a quiet state; tranquil; calm.
2. Order, harmony.
3. Without war.

God's peace starts with #3 above. Peace is "being without war." We lose our peace because there is a spiritual war going on inside us. War is present.

"Dearly beloved, I beseech you as strangers and pilgrims, abstain from fleshly lusts, which war against the soul." 1 Peter 2:11

God's answer to this is seen in His announcement of the Christ child by the angels. "Peace on earth, good will toward men." God wants to give you peace in your heart.

God became man to show you how to activate His
peace in your heart. He came as the Prince of
Peace! This is His official title. If you want to
understand peace, study Jesus. He won His battle
over the flesh, the eyes, and the pride of life when
He fasted for forty days in the wilderness at the
beginning of His ministry. From that time on, His
life was a life of servanthood. He lived His life for
the benefit of others (Matt. 20:28). When you have
no will of your own but delight in doing the will of
God, you are not offended when things do not
work out your way. You are at peace with God.

Our primary need in life is to discover and
understand oneself. There are problems that arise
because we are ignorant about who we are. We are
ignorant about how we are put together. We are
eternal souls that will live forever, somewhere. The
eternal soul has been placed in a body of flesh.
These two parts are at war with each other. The
flesh wars against the soul. The soul wars against
the flesh. They are contrary to each other.

In Galatians 5:17, Paul writes, "For the flesh
lusteth against the Spirit, and the Spirit against the
flesh: and these are contrary the one to the other:
so that ye cannot do the things that ye would."

It is a battle for survival every time. Only one can win. If the flesh wins the battle, there is no peace. If the soul wins the battle, then God will reward you with His peace.

"Dearly beloved, I beseech you as strangers and pilgrims, abstain from fleshly lusts, which war against the soul." 1 Peter 2:11

We can never satisfy the flesh. Many times in life we lose our peace because we do not realize we have the power to keep our peace. We turn it loose because of the weakness of the flesh. We may feel threatened or perhaps our pride has been hurt. We say things that come back to haunt us. In the end, we are sorry that we didn't hold our peace. Then, we are at war with our

> We lose our peace because we do not realize we have the power to keep our peace.

flesh for the stupid blunder we just made. The truth is, we can hold our peace in the most trying circumstances. But in order to activate God's peace, we must learn how to win the war against our flesh

31

We need to know God and His ways.

"But let him that glorieth glory in this, that he understandeth and knoweth me, that I am the LORD which exercise loving kindness, judgment, and righteousness, in the earth: for in these things I delight, saith the LORD." Jeremiah 9:24

It is our soul that needs God's peace in it. There can be no peace in our souls until this spiritual war is won. When you win this spiritual war, God's peace will flood your soul. Then, you will be in a state of order and harmony with God. You will be at peace. You will have conquered your flesh by bringing it under the control of the Spirit of God. Then, you will be one with God. You will no longer be fighting to have your own way in the flesh. God's peace will be in your life.

"For whatsoever is born of God overcometh the world: and this is the victory that overcometh the world, even our faith." 1 John 5:4

What is the peace of God? Here is "The Peace of God" as told by the scriptures. The New Living Translation calls the peace of God, **God's Peace**.

In Philippians 4:6-7, Paul writes, "Don't worry about anything; instead, pray about everything. Tell God what you need, and thank him for all he has done. If you do this, you will experience **God's peace**, which is far more wonderful than the human mind can understand. His peace will guard your hearts and minds as you live in Christ Jesus."

These verses in the King James Version calls it **"The Peace of God"** from which our title was taken. "Be careful for nothing; but in every thing by prayer and supplication with thanksgiving let your requests be known unto God. And **the peace of God**, which passeth all understanding, will keep your hearts and minds through Christ Jesus."

I personally like the King James formula for activating the peace of God in my life. It starts by saying, "Be careful for nothing." So, just blurt out your problem. God is your Father. He pities you as His child. He does not expect perfection in your approach to Him. He wants you to have and expects you to have the spirit of a trusting child.

He wants you to come to Him as your Father, believing He loves you. He invites you to come to Him with all the rights and wrongs in your situation. He will sort them out and show you what is right. Then, He will wipe the tears from your eyes and give you a new start with His peace, displacing your worry. He wants you to come to Him as a child with all the rights of inheritance. My mind tells me, "Give God what He wants."

The Peace of God

Chapter 5

The Peace of God in Finances

God is concerned with our finances. Why should we worry when we can pray instead? There is much in the Bible about the wealth of the righteous. Properly understood, wealth is something God gives us the power to get. He does this so that we may set up His covenant on the earth (Deut. 8:18). Rightly regarded, we can become a blessing to the nations with our wealth. This door is wide open to God's people. It's just that the eyes of our understanding have to be opened to it.

There is a wide range of wealth in the people of God. It ranges from poor to wealthy. They all are a part of His program on earth. He does not want anyone in this wide range to worry about money. The rich have big money problems. The poor have big money problems. There is no difference. We all need to trust and obey God. Nothing is too hard for the Lord.

"Ah Lord GOD! Behold, thou hast made the heaven and the earth by thy great power and stretched out arm, and there is nothing too hard for thee." Jeremiah 32:17

"But my God will supply all your need according to his riches in glory by Christ Jesus." Philippians 4:19

"For the poor always ye have with you." John 12:8

"Hearken, my beloved brethren, Hath not God chosen the poor of this world rich in faith, and heirs of the kingdom which he hath promised to them that love him?" James 2:5

"And the poor have the gospel preached to them." Matthew 11:5

The Gospel is the "good news." The poor need to have the good news preached to them. The good news to the poor is that "They do not have to be poor anymore."

Money is deceitful. The deceitfulness of riches will choke the word of God in your life and you will become unproductive. Greed has destroyed many people.

Now, the truth of the matter is few people have money problems. They have "MONEY MANAGEMENT PROBLEMS." STOP! Think about what I just said until you fully comprehend it.

I once had some money management problems. I owned rental properties and I got behind in a payment because of one of the properties. The Building and Loan was going to foreclose on me. I was feeling bad because I did not want that to happen. I was caught in a money management problem.

I prayed and prayed about it. They were going to foreclose on Thursday. On Monday I renewed my faith in God by saying: "IT'S NOT THURSDAY YET!" I then had my strength for Monday. I had no money, just faith in God. Tuesday came. I renewed my faith with the same words: "IT'S NOT THURSDAY YET!" Wednesday came. I renewed my faith with the same words: "IT'S NOT THURSDAY YET!" Before Wednesday was over the Building and Loan called. They said, "We are not going to foreclose, instead we are going to loan you more money."

Think about that. When I was praying, not knowing how God was going to answer, He was generating "FAVOR FOR ME" in their hearts.

They loaned me more money on another property. I was able to pay my back payments and continue my real estate business. I learned from their FAVOR that sometimes that is all we need. FAVOR will take us through our trials in life until we can perform our duty again.

When money is involved your flesh can never be satisfied. Wisdom says if you have food and clothes, you should be content. Beyond our basic needs we should live within our means. Your finances are like a pie. You can cut the pie into as many pieces as you want but the pie never gets bigger. The pieces just get smaller. You are taking away from something to do something else.

It's like missing a payment on the automobile so you can place a down payment on a boat. You are creating a money management problem when you do this. It would be nice if we could learn this without going through it, but experience is the better teacher. It is harsh, but we remember the pain.

THE PARABLE OF THE MONEY JUNKIE

Once upon a time, not so long ago, there was a money junkie. He loved money and he loved to spend money. He just could not save. When he got money in his hands, he just had to spend it. He would get restless. He couldn't sit still. The only thing on his mind was that money. So he would go out and spend it all.

The next morning he would wake up with what is called "buyer's remorse." He didn't want what he bought and now he was feeling sorry for himself. The money was all gone. He had to have another fix.

With his head in his hands, he started to think and he said to himself, "I am like a person on dope. I am a money junkie and I can't help myself. I can't continue like this. I must change. I am ashamed when I think of all the money I have handled in my lifetime and look at how little I have to show for it. Surely I can do better." Then, he designed a plan.

When he started to look around, he saw his problem. Many of the people around him were also money junkies. They were all spending all they had. He was just one of the gang.

Then, he went to the store to get a loaf of bread. As he looked around the store, he saw the shelves stocked with food. He saw many people coming with money to buy the food. He went to the storekeeper and asked, "How can I become a storekeeper like you?"

The storekeeper's answer was simple but it was a breakthrough for the money junkie. The owner said, "Don't spend all of your money. Save! Invest some of it so it can work for you. You will have to start small and it will take time, but you can do it."

The money junkie's small vision was expanded with that simple, blockbusting statement. He thought, "That's remarkable, amazing."

The storekeeper continued, "The money I have saved is invested in what you see on the shelves. The customers are giving me more money for the products than I paid for them. After I pay my bills, I buy more food for the shelves with the profit. Someday soon I'm going to do what others can't afford to do. I will travel while my son runs the store. Then, he will learn how I did it. One day, he, too, will be able to do what others can't afford to do."

The money junkie paid the man for his bread and said, "Thank you, Sir. You have helped me." He went home and devised a better plan than the storekeeper had given him. He found a way that **low-income people** could get ahead. He kicked the money-junkie habit and became successful.

To take advantage of what you just read, here is what you need to do. Look at where you are with your finances. What is your income? That's it. That's all there is.

Design a plan around the most important things for which you are willing to spend your money. Number one is the cost of where you will live including the utilities. Number two is your food. Number three is what you will wear. Then, work out a plan from there. Manage your money. If you want more money, design a plan on how you will get it. Don't be foolish spending the rent money on something else. Live within your means or lose your peace!

I have written a book on God's plan for how to get ahead in life. The title is "A Light Shining Out of Darkness." Its basis is God's plan found in Genesis chapter one. God spoke the end from the beginning. He could declare His end because He had spoken a master plan that He would work by until it was finished.

You can plan your life the same way by using the same principles God had for His plan. My book will give you the details you need in order to follow this plan. When you use this plan, God becomes your partner because it is His plan that you are using.

God's seven-step plan began in Genesis 1:1, the first day. The work on the first day made things ready for the work on the second day. God listed everything to be done on each day for seven days. Then He went to work. He finished the things written in His plan. God is not done yet. He is still working on us.

You need God's plan for your life. A plan will manage your finances. It will help you get ahead so you can help others. The poor can't help the poor. God needs you to help them.

The Gospel (good news) is that the poor do not have to be poor anymore. That alone should bring God's peace into your heart today. If you are poor, look to God. If you have money, you have an opportunity to give to the poor. The Bible teaches that when you give to the poor, you are lending to the LORD. God has chosen the poor of this world to be rich in faith.

The key is found in Hebrews 13:5-6. "Let your conversation be without covetousness; and be content with such things as ye have: for he hath said, I will never leave thee, nor forsake thee. So that we may boldly say, 'The Lord is my helper, and I will not fear what man will do unto me.'"

You can get ahead. God wants you to get ahead. You must study and plan on how to do it.

The Peace of God

Chapter 6

The Peace of God in the Storm

I am happy to tell you that the peace of God can displace your worry right in the beginning of your problem if you activate it. This will work for you. With this book and your Bible you can activate the peace of God in your life and even get better at it as time goes on. I want to tell you a story found in the Bible. It is about a severe storm on the Sea of Galilee. Peace is stilling the storm and taking away the problem.

The Day the Wind Ran out of Breath

"And the same day, when the even was come, he saith unto them, 'Let us pass over unto the other side.' And when they had sent away the multitude, they took him even as he was in the ship. And there were also with him other little ships. And there arose a great storm of wind, and the waves beat into the ship, so that it was full. And he was in the hinder part of the ship, asleep on a pillow: and they awake him, and say unto him, 'Master, carest thou not that we perish?' And he arose, and rebuked the wind, and said unto the sea, '**Peace, be still.**' And the wind stopped, and there was a great calm. And he said unto them, 'Why are ye so fearful? How is it that ye have no faith?' And they feared exceedingly, and said one to another, 'What manner of man is this, that even **the wind and the sea obey him?'** Mark 4:35-41

This same story in The Message Bible reads as follows:

THE WIND RAN OUT OF BREATH
"Late that day he said to them, 'Let us go across to the other side.' They took him in the boat as he was. Other boats came along. A huge storm came up. Waves poured into the boat, threatening to sink it. And Jesus was in the stern, head on a pillow, sleeping! They roused him, saying, 'Teacher, is it nothing to you that we're going down?' Awake, he told the wind to pipe down and said to the sea, 'Quiet! Settle down!' The wind ran out of breath; the sea became smooth as glass. Jesus reprimanded the disciples: 'Why are you such cowards? Have you no faith at all?' They were in absolute awe, staggered. 'Who is this, anyway?' they asked. 'Wind and sea at his beck and call!'"

Please picture this storm in your mind. Project

yourself into that boat with them. Feel the fear of losing your life because of the storm. Watch as they awake Jesus. See and hear Him speak the words, "Peace be still." Experience the joy of the wind and the sea obeying Him. The noise stops as the wind stops. The boat settles down on calm water and you are left with Jesus still in the boat. You are feeling that everything is all right again. A wonderful, peaceful feeling comes over you. You feel grateful to Jesus for performing a miracle.

Understand this story and all the emotions that come with it. That will give you an understanding of this book. This book is designed to work for you in the same way. In every storm you will ever have, Jesus will be present with you.

God is a Spirit. God is everywhere. There is no moment in your history that God is not there with you. He is ready when you are. The part of God that fills the space around you is on a stand-by notice

There cannot be a moment in your history that God is not there with you.

for you. Nothing can fill the space around you but God. It is as though you are the only one in the entire universe that He has to take care of. Give God what He wants. Believe this! Activate God's peace in your life.

Here is a warning, however. If you *know* the word but do not *do* the word, God's word will have no effect on your peace. You are saying that your thought process is stronger than God's word and that you can work it out on your own.

The two keys to getting a Bible promise are faith and obedience. You must hear the word, believe the promise is for you, and then do the work that God has assigned to it. Jesus said, "He that heareth these sayings of mine and doeth them, he is a wise man" (Matt. 7:24)
To activate God's peace in your life you must do the following:
1. Believe there is a God.
2. Believe in His integrity. He cannot lie. His word He will do.
3. Believe in His peace covenant with you.
4. Believe that He loves you with an everlasting love.
5. Believe that He rewards them that diligently seek Him.
6. Believe all this in your troubled heart.

"If my people, which are called by my name, shall humble themselves, and pray, and seek my face, and turn from their wicked ways; then will I hear from heaven, and will forgive their sin, and will heal their land." 2 Chronicles 7:14

"For thus saith the LORD, 'Behold, I will extend peace to her like a river.'" Isaiah 66:12

"When a man's ways please the LORD, he maketh even his enemies to be at peace with him." Proverbs 16:7

When you are obeying God's word something happens. His peace flows in like a river. You will be amazed at how peaceful you feel even though you still have all your problems. Embedded in your system is the affirmation, "Everything is going to be all right." He is the God of peace! He is the King of peace! He is the Prince of peace! These are His titles. He loves you so much. He wants you to cast all your cares on Him for He cares for you.

STOP! Don't just read on. Do it! Give God what He wants. Let Him love you. Cast your cares on Jesus. He loves you and wants you to do it.

The Peace of God

Chapter 7

How We Can Control Satan

Let me give you some insights regarding our fight against Satan. Satan is not the all-powerful one.

"Ye are of God, little children, and have overcome them: because greater is he that is in you, than he that is in the world." 1 John 4:4

> Satan is not the greater one. The greater one is in you.

The Greater One is in us.

"And we do know that we know him, if we keep his commandments." 1 John 2:3

In doing battle with Satan you must know how he fights. In 2 Corinthians 2:11, the Apostle Paul said: "We are not ignorant of his devices." The Greek word here, which is translated "devices," is the same Greek word that is translated "thought" in 2 Corinthians 10:5, "bringing every thought into captivity." So Satan attacks us through our thoughts. Our ability to control Satan lies in our ability to control our thoughts. "Resist the devil's thoughts and he will flee from you. Draw nigh unto God's thoughts and He will draw nigh unto you." James 4:7-8.

How to Perform That Which is Good

"For I know that in me (that is, in my flesh,) dwelleth no good thing: for to will is present with me; but how to perform that which is good I find not (in my flesh)." Romans 7:18

"I find then a law, that, when I would do good, evil is present with me." Romans 7:21

The dilemma we have lies in our control. I want to do right, but there is another side of me warring against my doing the good. We must learn how to overcome evil with good.

There are three things involved. First, there is my mind that wants to do right. Second, there is my flesh that wants to do evil. And finally, there is my enemy, Satan, who wants to destroy me. Satan is not the greater one. The greater one, God, is in me. I will treat Satan like he is a liar.

We control Satan by obeying God's Word. This control can be compared to our control over nature. We obey the rules of nature. If we want good health, we get into the sunshine. We let it do its work. If we want healthy blood, we breathe fresh air. If we want a clean system, we drink good water. If we want endurance, we build muscle through exercising. We obey the rules.

We Control Satan by Resisting him As a Liar

"Ye are of your father the devil, and the lusts of your father ye will do. He was a murderer from the beginning, and abode not in the truth, because there is no truth in him. When he speaketh a lie, he speaketh of his own: for he is a liar, and the father of it." John 8:44

It is with spiritual rules we control Satan. We let God be true. We obey God's Word. When we do this, we control Satan by showing him to be a liar. He is a "lie's" father. He cannot overcome God's Word .We can endure whatever Satan puts on us with

> We control Satan by resisting him as a liar.

God's peace. This peace passes all understanding. The Truth has set us free.

"Knowing that whatsoever good thing a man doeth, the same will he receive of the Lord, whether he be bond or free." Ephesians 6:8

The truth is that God is not willing that one person should perish (2 Pet. 3:9). He extends His love to all. He lets the sun rise on the evil and the good. Whatever good thing I do for a man is right in God's eyes. He will do the same for me (Eph. 6:8). That's a promise in His word. So, because I am obeying the scripture, I have control over Satan's false feeling. I have control over this feeling of remorse that he is trying to inflict on me. When I rebuke him I command him to leave. The feeling has to go. I will let God be true. I will give God what He wants.

Wisdom Anchors You

"If any of you lack wisdom, let him ask of God, that giveth to all men liberally, and upbraideth not; and it will be given him. But let him ask in faith, nothing wavering. For he that wavereth is like a wave of the sea driven with the wind and tossed. For let not that man think that he will receive a thing of the Lord. A double minded man is unstable in all his ways." James 1:5-8

To have God's peace in your heart's biggest

problem, you must work at removing all unbelief from your mind. If you do not do this, you are double-minded, unstable in all your ways. (See James 1:8 above.)

"Casting down imaginations, and every high thing that exalteth itself against the knowledge of God, and bringing into captivity every thought to the obedience of Christ." 2 Corinthians 10:5

This battle is won by bringing every thought into captivity. Thoughts are things we need to manage and control. You must not let your thoughts run away with you. You should control every thought that is in your mind either by awareness or by default. You forfeit your control by letting your mind think on anything but God's words.

You control by awareness when you fill your mind with God's promises from the Bible. The Bible is God's Living Word. He is alive speaking His word from the Bible directly into your heart today.

You are miraculously at peace when you know God loves you in your heart's biggest problem. When you accept His word as truth, it becomes God living in you. Remember, fear is from Satan and God's word drives out fear.

The Peace of God

Chapter 8

Obey Until It Happens

Let me explain just what I mean when I say we are to obey it until it clearly happens. The first thing we must do is discover the promise in God's word about the peace of God that we need. After this, we must treat God's promise as a seed. Next, we plant this seed in our heart and let it grow for as long as is needed for this seed to produce its fruit.

This will result in the promise becoming real in our troubled lives because we have activated the peace of God that is promised in His word. We have obeyed the word until it clearly happens. The peace of God now reigns in our heart.

Jesus explained it like this in Mark 4:26-29, "And he said, 'So is the kingdom of God, is like a man should cast seed into the ground; And should sleep, and rise night and day, and the seed should spring and grow up, **he knoweth not how.** For the earth bringeth forth fruit of herself; first the blade, then the ear, after that the full corn in the ear. But when the fruit is brought forth, immediately he putteth in the sickle, because the harvest is come.'"

We do not know everything that went on in our hearts when the seed was planted. We just know we have the fruit of the seed planted, "The Peace of God."

Allow me to refer again to Philippians 4:7. "And the peace of God, which passeth all understanding, shall keep your hearts and minds through Christ Jesus."

The peace of God will keep your hearts. The word "keep" here is the Greek word phroureo. It has these meanings:

1. To be a watcher in advance
2. To mount guard as a sentinel
3. Post spies at gates
4. To hem in
5. Protect: Keep (with a garrison).

The peace of God is doing all this for your heart and mind through Christ Jesus. This is why God's peace passes all understanding. Don't try to understand it. Just believe it, obey it, and teach others by your example. Reinforce and maintain your peaceful dominion.

The Early Church Maintained Their Peace by "Continuing Steadfastly"

"And they continued steadfastly in the apostles' doctrine and fellowship, and in breaking of bread, and in <u>prayers.</u>" Acts 2:42

The knowledge of how to think and act in the time of our biggest problem comes through the man, Christ Jesus. Jesus came to be a doer of the word and to give us an example for

> **Study Jesus' life and imitate Him.**

living. Study Jesus' life and imitate Him. Do good. He is a Prince at this. He kept His peace when they all forsook Him.

You Should Teach Others How to Obey God's Word.

"Teaching them to observe all things whatsoever I have commanded you: and, lo, I am with you alway, even unto the end of the world. Amen." Matthew 28:20

You are never alone in this. He is always with you and always there to help you.

You Should Teach Others How to Observe

The Greek word for "observe" is tereo (tay-reh'-o) and has the following meanings:

1. A watch.
2. To guard (from loss or injury, properly, by keeping the eye on).
3. To prevent escaping.
4. A fortress or full military lines of apparatus.
5. To note (a prophecy; figuratively, to fulfill a command).
6. By implication, to detain (in custody; figuratively, to maintain).
7. Hold fast, keep (-er), (pre-, re-) serve, watch.

The dictionary meaning of "observe" is "To conform one's action or practice to; comply with; as, to *observe* the rules."

Observing is obeying. Meditate day and night on the verse with your promise. Stop being self conscious and release your spirit. Just speak it aloud.

"Be careful for nothing; but in every thing by prayer and supplication with thanksgiving let your requests be made known unto God."
Philippians 4:6

Put your future in the hands of God. That is a safe and peaceful place to be. Become hidden in Christ by taking no thought about the outcome of your problem. Word your way out. Let the word do the work without interfering with it. Only believe.

The psalmist said it this way, "Wait on the LORD: be of good courage, and he shall strengthen thine heart: wait, I say, on the LORD." Psalm 27:14

Spiritual Rules are Different

You must think spiritually! In the temporal world you can "reason" with things and think them through. But when you "reason" with your own mind in the spiritual

You cannot second guess God.

world, you are trying to second guess what God is doing. That's confusing. You cannot do that.

God's plan for your life is so much bigger than you can comprehend. God has such a big picture for your life that you will never see it all. Your life in the spiritual world is to TRUST and OBEY. There is no other way.

You must trust God. Just keep walking in His promises. He is there! Obey the word completely and things will get clearer. He is ALWAYS with you!

How to Advance and Obey

This means to accept God's promise as God's will for your life. Delight yourself in doing His will. The obstacles will have to go. God's promise will remain as long as you do not allow the cares of this life to choke the word.

"And the cares of this world, and the deceitfulness of riches, and the lusts of other things entering in, choke the word, and it becometh unfruitful."
Mark 4:19

"Casting all your care on him; for he careth for you." 1 Peter 5:7

Do not be concerned that you are not getting your way because He is looking out for you. Think like a child. Tell yourself, "My father will take care of this."

Observe the rules. Conform to the rules. Comply with the rules. Guard your peaceful dominion with His peace.

Use These Affirmation Confessions

"I have kept My Father's commandments."
John 15:8-11

"I delight to do thy will, O my God: yea, thy law is in my heart." Psalm 40:8

"Blessed is the man that walketh not in the counsel of the ungodly, nor standeth with sinners, nor sitteth in the seat of the scornful. But his delight is in the law of the LORD; and in his law doth he meditate day and night." Psalm 1:1-2

"Encourage me to go in thy commandments; for in it do I delight." Psalm 119:35

"Let thy tender mercies come unto me, that I may live: for thy law is my delight." Psalm 119:77

"But let him that glorieth glory in this, that he understandeth and knoweth me, that I am the LORD that exercise loving kindness, judgment, and righteousness, in the earth: for in these things I delight, saith the LORD." Jeremiah 9:24

"I find then a law, that, when I would do good, evil is present with me. For I delight in the law of God after the inward man." Romans 7:21-22

The Peace of God

Chapter 9

What Releases God's Promises

When you accept God's word as truth, it becomes God living in you. Fear is from Satan. God's love for you drives out fear. You are miraculously at peace when you know that God loves you in

> When you accept God's word as truth it becomes God living in you.

your heart's biggest problem. You have come to the place when you release your spirit to Him. You turn it all over to God. The outcome is now in God's hands. Whatever happens is His will.

You have just learned that the opposite of love is not hate but fear. The opposite of fear is love, and God has cast out all fear with His love.

The soil releases the promise in the seed. When good seed is planted in moist, fertile soil the seed will put its demands on that soil and release the promise of God in it. Prepare your heart for this.

Experience the Integrity of God's Word
by Obeying

Continue to obey God's word until the promise is made manifest. When you are made aware of a promise in the Bible, you are also made aware of the discipline needed to get it. Knowledge is discipline. This is true in everything you try to do. You must be a doer of your knowledge. The world is full of dreamers who will never accomplish their dreams. They are not putting action to what they know they need to do.

You must be a doer of your knowledge.
Answer these two questions.
What do I know? Do I do what I know?

"He answered and said, 'Whether he be a sinner or no, I know not: **one thing I know**, that, though I was blind, I see.'" John 9:25

"Brethren, I count not myself to have apprehended: but this **one thing I do**, forgetting those things that are behind, and reaching forth unto those things that are before, **I press** toward the mark for the prize of the high calling of God in Christ Jesus. **Let us** thus, as many as be perfect, be thus minded: and if in a thing ye be otherwise minded, God will show even this unto you. But, whereto we have already gained, **let us walk** by the same rule, **let us mind** the same thing. Brethren, be followers together of me, and mark them that walk so as ye have us for an example. Philippians 3:13-17

Look at the highlighted words I have lined up.
One thing I know
One thing I do
I press
Let us
Let us walk
Let us mind
I like the way they line up and the pattern they make. They are all inspired scripture.

We always possess a vision of the promise before it becomes real to us. What releases this promise of God that we see in our vision? To obey it clearly we must know about these things:

1. **The Law of the Offering**
2. **A New Covenant Relationship of Love**
3. **Know the Process**
4. **Set Obedience in Order**

1. The Law of the Offering

All people need to be loved. Our relationship with God is based on love. He likens it to the relationship between a man and his wife, whom he loves dearly. There is a romance going on in the universe right now. God is trying to get people to love Him. He is looking for His bride.

Love is the giving and receiving of gifts. God loves a cheerful giver (2 Cor. 9:7). You activate the wonderful love of God in your life when you give to His work on the earth. God loves a cheerful

> God loves a cheerful giver. God will take care of a cheerful giver.

giver. He will take care of the person who loves Him enough to give to His cause. In order to release the peace of God in your life, give a generous offering to Him. God will love you for it. He will make all grace abound toward you in everything.

"And God is able to make all grace abound toward you; that ye, always having all sufficiency in all things, may abound to every good work."
2 Corinthians 9:8

Give your tithes which is a tenth of all your income.

"'Bring ye all the tithes into the storehouse, that there may be meat in mine house, and prove me,

saith the LORD of hosts, if I will not open you the windows of heaven, and pour you out a blessing, that there will not be room enough to receive it. And I will rebuke the devourer for your sakes, and he will not destroy the fruits of your ground; neither will your vine cast her fruit before the time in the field,' saith the LORD of hosts."
Malachi 3:10-11

Notice the word "windows" is plural. That means there are many windows. The law of the offering is based on the desire of a willing mind. You desire to give your love back to God. God shows you who has his blessing for you. He will show you what you didn't see before. He will show you how to get it.

"Have faith in God." Mark 11:22

"God loves a cheerful giver." 2 Corinthians 9:7

Worship God in giving. Every time you give, whatever you give, and to whomever you give, worship God.

"Through faith and patience inherit the promises." Hebrews 6:12

This is the LAW of the offering.

2. A New Covenant Relationship of Love

The Law lacked one thing, "A Perfect sacrifice." The blood of bulls and goats could not take away sin; thus, sin was remembered again every year on

> The ransom for sin has been paid. We are FREE.

the Day of Atonement (Heb. 10:4). God put His perfect sacrifice on hold until Jesus came. Jesus was God's New Covenant of Love.

Jesus fulfilled the law. What the Law could not do, Jesus did. He paid the sin offering in full. It is finished! The ransom has been paid. We can be free at last. We prove the fulfilled Law. When we receive the peace of God at the level of our biggest problem, we prove that the Law has been fulfilled. Sin no longer has dominion over us.

"Do we then void the law through faith? God forbid: yea, we prove the law." Romans 3:31

I prove the law by believing and receiving His Righteousness by faith. I love Him by keeping His commandments. I become an established fact that the law is fulfilled.

I am the law fulfilled.

I am the righteousness of Christ.
I am in Christ.
I am justified by faith.

All this has been imputed to me by the righteousness of my faith in God. (Rom. 4:22-25).

By my faith God has released His Promise to me. This is the law of faith about justification. God is justified in doing this because He died for my sins.

"Therefore being justified by faith, we have peace with God through our Lord Jesus Christ: by whom also we have access by faith into this grace wherein we stand, and rejoice in hope of the glory of God." Romans 5:1-2

"Finally, be ye all of one mind, having compassion one of another, love as brethren, be pitiful, be courteous: Not giving evil for evil, or railing for railing: but contrariwise blessing; knowing that ye are thereunto called, that ye should inherit a blessing. For he that will love life, and see good days, let him refrain his tongue from evil, and his lips that they speak no guile: Let him avoid evil, and do good; let him seek peace, and ensue it."
1 Peter 3:8-11

This is our new covenant relationship of love.

"We love Him because He first loved us with an everlasting love." 1 John 4:19

"But God commendeth his love toward us, in that, while we were yet sinners, Christ died for us." Romans 5:8

"Hereby perceive we the love of God, because he laid down his life for us: and we ought to lay down our lives for the brethren." 1 John 3:16

3. Know the Process

Step One is God and His love

The peace of God is the love of God. This is the beginning knowledge of the process.

Step Two is Our perception and reception

We perceive the love of God in the picture of the cross. He loved us enough to lay down His life for us. Some people are blind and cannot perceive this. We must believe the strong love God has for us. It is His love that replaces our "fear of losing" with His peace.

Step Three is Our response: Faith, Obedience

Once we perceive the love of God, we are inspired by faith to be obedient to 1 Peter 5:7. "Casting all your care upon him; for he careth for you." This is a leap of faith. We must give God what He wants.

Step Four is Our reward: The Peace of God

Without faith it cannot be done.

"But without faith it is impossible to please him: for he that cometh to God must believe that he is, and that he is a rewarder of them that diligently seek him." Hebrews 11:6

4. Set Obedience in Order

Without wisdom and understanding we are confused.

"Happy is the man that findeth wisdom, and the man that getteth understanding." Proverbs 3:13

"Wisdom is the chief thing; So get wisdom: and with all thy getting get understanding." Proverbs 4:7

We must understand the wisdom of laying hold on God's word and obeying it.

> Wisdom is laying hold on God's word and with faith obeying it.

******

"She is a tree of life to them that lay hold on her: and happy is every one that retaineth her." Proverbs 3:18

Obey, by laying hold on wisdom. Put a demand on her seed by believing these words: "She is a tree of life."

******

"For the eyes of the Lord are over the righteous, and his ears are open unto their prayers: but the face of the Lord is against them that do evil." 1 Peter 3:12

Obey by laying hold on wisdom. Put a demand on her seed by believing these words: "The eyes of the Lord are over the righteous." Also, in this same verse it says, "His ears are open unto their prayers."

Obey by laying hold on wisdom. Put a demand on her seed by believing these words: "<u>His ears are open unto their prayers.</u>"

******

"Who<u> will give to every man according to his deeds.</u>" Romans 2:6

Obey by laying hold of wisdom. Put a demand on her seed by believing these words: "<u>Who will give to every man according to his deeds.</u>"

******

"And if we know that he hear us, whatsoever we ask, we know that <u>we have the petitions that we desired </u>of him." 1 John 5:15

Obey by laying hold of wisdom. Put a demand on her seed by believing these words: <u>"We have the petitions that we desired."</u>

******

And this is the confidence that we have in him, that <u>if we ask a thing according to his will, he heareth us."</u> 1 John 5:14

Obey by laying hold of wisdom. Put a demand on her seed by believing these words: <u>"If we ask anything according to his will, he heareth us."</u>

******

"And <u>we do know that we know </u>him, if we keep his commandments." 1 John 2:3

Obey by laying hold of wisdom. Put a demand on her seed by believing these words: <u>"We do know that we know.</u>

******

"With good will doing service, to the Lord, and not to men: Knowing that whatsoever good thing a man doeth, the same will he receive of the Lord, whether he be bond or free." (No respecter of persons) Ephesians 6:7

Obey by laying hold on wisdom. Put a demand on her seed by believing these words: "<u>Knowing that whatsoever good thing a man doeth, the same will he receive of the Lord, whether he be bond or free.</u>"

Summary

You must want the peace of God or it will not happen. Want is the key.

The peace of God is a gift. You must receive it as a gift or you will do without.

The peace of God is given to you because He loves you.

"O the depth of the riches both of the wisdom and knowledge of God! How unsearchable are his judgments, and his ways past finding out!" Romans 11:33

"God's judgments are unsearchable and His ways past finding out."

"And the peace of God, that passeth all understanding, will keep your hearts and minds through Christ Jesus." Philippians 4:7

The peace of God passeth all understanding.

Don't try to understand it. You cannot do it.
You can only believe it and obey it.

You cannot force it out of God.
You can only obey it completely.

Meditate day and night.

Word your way out of your turmoil. Have faith
in God's word.

**The paradox in this is that it is easy to
understand and hard to do, while it is hard to
understand and easy to do.**

Things to Remember

1. The Golden Rule is no respecter of persons.
   Do good unto others.

2. The law of sowing and reaping is no respecter
   of persons. Sow the right seed.

3. Lay hold of wisdom, **sow her seed,** and you
   will have the want of your heart.

4. Believe and **YOU** will receive the peace of
   God in your biggest problem.